Mockingbird

The Mockingbird is noted for its ability to imitate the songs of many other birds. They are often heard singing during the night and very early in the morning. From a distance, it is easily recognized by its general gray coloration and conspicuous white areas on the wings. Look for it in cities and around old ranch houses. The Mockingbird is the State Bird of Texas.

Black-chinned Hummingbird

This species is best identified by the blackish throat which has a white area underneath. While it is one of our most common "hummers," it is more likely to be found in cities or other areas where trees are numerous. Don't look for it on the open desert. Hummingbirds are our smallest birds. Only the males possess the colorful throat patches; the females are more drab in appearance and often difficult to identify.

Desert Birds: An Introduction

The Southwestern deserts have a wide variety of habitats which are occupied by many different species of birds. Some of the birds that occur are found nowhere else in the United States.

These deserts have many interesting species which are adapted to life in hot, arid environments. Included in this guide are most of the more common species—the ones you are likely to encounter in a desert city or in open desert areas. Desert birds are usually best observed early in the morning. Once the heat of the day sets in, they are less active.

This *Easy Field Guide*® is part of a series of pocket guides to the more interesting common species of desert plants and critters. A checklist is included in the back of this book so you may keep a record of the birds you observe.

Three "State Birds" are described in this book and commonly seen throughout the Southwestern deserts: Arizona's Cactus Wren, New Mexico's Roadrunner and Texas' Mockingbird. The Gambel's Quail, a close cousin to the California Quail, the State Bird of California, is also described herein.

Cactus Wren

The Cactus Wren's somewhat ratchety song is heard throughout much of the day in many desert areas. Besides being large for a wren, note the dark spots on the breast. Often seen running under shrubbery, their large nests are often found snuggled into a cholla cactus. They may build several nests during the breeding season. Common in towns and cities, the Cactus Wren is Arizona's State Bird.

Costa's Hummingbird

In contrast to the Black-chinned Hummingbird which seems to require trees, the Costa's can be found out on the open desert. Look for it in the spring; it migrates to the West Coast soon after. The Costa's has a violet-covered area on top of the head, and the similarly-colored throat has feathers which extend out and back. It is often seen feeding on the bright, red-orange blossoms of the ocotillo. As with other hummingbirds, its food consists primarily of nectar from flowers and of small insects.

Ash-throated Flycatcher

Flycatchers include a group of birds which typically sit on an exposed perch and fly out to catch passing insects. Usually, they return to the same or a nearby perch. The Ash-throated is one of our more common fly-catchers. Look for the reddish-brown tail, a hint of yellow on the belly and two faint bars on the wings. We have often seen its nesting hole in a yucca stalk.

Black-tailed Gnatcatcher

This small bird often goes unnoticed as it works its way through trees and shrubs in search of insects. It has a longish appearance for its size, and the undertail is mostly black with a white area on each side. The upper body color is a sort of grayish blue, and the underparts are light. It seems to be rather common in dry desert washes where vegetation grows.

Loggerhead Shrike

At first sight, you might confuse this species with the similarly-colored Mockingbird; but other than both having gray and white on their bodies, the similarity ends. Shrikes catch insects and even mice and have been known to impale these on mesquite thorns and barbed wire. With their food "tied down," they can tear it apart more easily. Shrikes are most often encountered perched in a low tree or shrub. Note the fast wing beats and tendency to fly low over they ground. At close range, note the black mask on the face and the short powerful bill.

Hooded Oriole

The Hooded Oriole is one of the most attractive of the desert birds. The yellow-orange area on top of its head will separate it from the other common oriole, the Northern Oriole. In the latter, the top of the head has considerable black. The tail of the Hooded is black. Look for this species in areas where cottonwoods grow. Another oriole that you might see in the desert areas is the Scott's Oriole. Instead of being yellow-orange and black, it is bright yellow and black.

Cardinal

The brilliant red of the male and the pinkish bill of both sexes will separate the Cardinal from the only other bird it is likely to be confused with, the Pyrrhuloxia. The male Cardinal also has a black area on its face surrounding the bill. Cardinals are often found in cities.

Pyrrhuloxia

Both the Pyrrhuloxia and the Cardinal have crests, but the Pyrrhuloxia has a yellowish bill while that of the Cardinal is pink. The Pyrrhuloxia also tends to have a lot of gray on its body. Look for it in shrubby areas.

Phainopepla

This interesting bird can often be spotted as you drive down the highway. Look for a black bird (the male) with a crest, perched at the top of a mesquite. When the bird flies, the white area on each wing will cinch the identification. One of its favorite foods is the white-colored berry of the mistletoe, a plant common in many desert regions. It feeds on insects which it catches on the wing.

Purple Martin

This large swallow is sometimes very conspicuous around desert cities during the fall. Large numbers congregate near homes where they pose sort of a problem because of their droppings. This species often nests in desert trees and tall cactus such as saguaro. The male is a dark bluish-black, the female is grayish. They feed largely on insects.

Curve-billed Thrasher

The orangish eye and downcurved bill will help identify this species. Its call resembles a whistle and is a common desert sound along with the calls of the Gambel's Quail and the Cactus Wren. Other than the bill and the eye, the body is rather drab gray. It seems to prefer areas where cholla cactus grow.

Verdin

A tiny grayish bird that flits around in mesquites may be the Verdin. A closer view will reveal a yellowish head if it is this species. Its unusual nest is often seen, consisting of a ball of dried vegetation with an entrance hole in the side rather than being the typical, cup-like nest of most birds.

Gambel's Quail

Similar to the California Quail, the Gambel's Quail is one of the more commonly seen desert birds. Its dark, curved topknot and plump body make it unmistakable. The Gambel's Quail prefers the company of others of its species, and coveys may include 20 or more birds. A drive along backcountry desert roads early in the morning will almost certainly result in your seeing many of these birds.

Roadrunner

This is the bird that desert visitors are most anxious to see—and they are seldom disappointed. It is a member of the cuckoo family. Preferring foot travel, it can fly and glide if pushed. Its diet consists largely of insects and, at times, snakes and lizards. You are most likely to see this bird as it crosses the road in front of your vehicle. The Roadrunner is New Mexico's State Bird.

White-winged Dove

This large dove is almost the size of the familiar domestic pigeon of many cities. When it flies, the large, white areas on the wings are very evident. Closer examination will also reveal smaller white areas on the tail.

Mourning Dove

The Mourning Dove is not as bulky as the White-winged Dove. In fact, it can often be recognized at fair distances by its long, tapered appearance and rapid flight. They are common in many areas. The general body coloration is grayish brown. Look for it along road shoulders where it feeds or gathers gravel. Its nest is a somewhat crude affair of sticks.

Common Flicker

Sometimes called the Gilded Flicker, these birds are large woodpeckers. They have a brown back, the underwings and tail are a brightly-colored yellow. As it flies away, note the white rump patch. This bird makes nesting holes in trees, utility poles and cereus cacti. A scar forms inside the cactus and leaves a cavity, locally called a "boot."

Gila Woodpecker

This noisy woodpecker can be found throughout the Southwest desert regions. Its unmusical call is a familiar desert sound. It is somewhat smaller than the Flicker, and its back has black and white horizontal stripes. Besides its call, it can be easily identified by the patch of white on each wing which it exhibits as it flies. Look for it along moist areas where trees such as cottonwoods grow.

Common Raven

Crows are usually not found in the desert, so the large black bird that you see circling over head or perched on a utility pole is likely to be the Common Raven. The Common Raven is found over much of North America, from cold mountain tops to the hot desert. The guttural call is an aid to identification.

Great Horned Owl

This large bird is often seen at dusk as it starts its nightly hunting forays. The large size and "horns" make it hard to confuse with any other bird. The Great Horned Owl is often the large bird which flies up at night from along the roadside. Its food consists largely of various species of mice, with an occasional larger animal such as a rabbit or skunk. The "who who" type of call is the easiest way to discover its presence. Like all predators, the Great Horned Owl is important in the desert ecosystem.

Screech Owl

This fascinating bird is our smallest owl to possess "horns" (actually feathers) on its head. While primarily nocturnal, it may occasionally be seen in the daytime at the entrance to its nest hole in a saguaro, cottonwood or other tree. We often know of its whereabouts by its calls at night—a series of sounds resembling the rhythm of a ball bouncing. It is not likely to be confused with our two other owls, the much larger Great Horned Owl and the tiny, "hornless" Elf Owl.

Elf Owl

The Elf Owl is the smallest species of owl in the United States. It nests in holes in trees and utility poles or as pictured here in a Saguaro cactus nesting hole pecked out by a Gila Woodpecker or perhaps a Common Flicker. Its food consists mainly of insects. At night, you can often locate it by listening for its calls.

Poor-will

As you drive down a dirt road in the desert during a spring or summer night, you are likely to see a big, somewhat nondescript bird flutter up in front of your headlights. Some people have likened the general appearance of its flight to that of a giant moth. More likely than not, what you have seen is a member of the Goatsucker family, the Poor-will. If you get out of your car and listen, you will hear others of this species as they call out "Poor-will" from the surrounding dark. They feed on flying insects. Note the bristles around the bill which aid in capturing this food.

Lesser Nighthawk

This species is not a hawk, although it may appear to be one at first. Note the long, pointed wings with white spots underneath. Flight often appears erratic as it goes by as low as 20 feet above ground. Attendance at a night outdoor event which is lighted will almost certainly result in seeing several of these birds as they fly around the floodlights catching insects. They belong to the same family as the Poor-will.

Red-tailed Hawk

A drive in the desert countryside will reveal many large hawks perched on utility poles or soaring in circles above. Perched, the Red-tail exhibits a whitish breast with a speckled band across it. In flight, the tail feathers show as a reddish-brown from underneath.

American Kestrel

The Kestrel (sometimes called the Sparrow Hawk) is our smallest species of hawk. Its favorite perch is atop a utility pole. We have seen many along some stretches of road. Sometimes they can be seen as they hover in one place, maybe 50 feet above the ground apparently in search of prey. The small size, along with the orangish-brown back, will aid in identification. Insects are their main food.

Turkey Vulture

Look above on any hot summer day, and you are likely to spot a large bird that soars and glides, seldom flapping its wings. If the front part of the underwings is darker than the rear part, the bird is most likely the Turkey Vulture. This is the so-called "buzzard" of western movies. Its primary food consists of dead animals. Vultures have amazing eyesight and can see for much greater distances than people can. At close range, note the small, reddish, bare head.

Checklist and Scientific Names

	Page
❏ **American Kestrel**—*Falco sparverius*	29
❏ **Ash-throated Flycatcher**—*Myiarchus cinerascens*	6
❏ **Black-chinned Hummingbird**—*Archilochus alexandri*	4
❏ **Black-tailed Gnatcatcher**—*Polioptila melanura*	7
❏ **Cactus Wren**—*Campylorhynchus brunneicapillum*	2
❏ **Cardinal**—*Cardinalis cardinalis*	10
❏ **Common Flicker**—*Colaptes auratus*	20
❏ **Common Raven**—*Corvus corax*	22
❏ **Costa's Hummingbird**—*Calypte costae*	5
❏ **Curve-billed Thrasher**—*Toxostoma curvirostre*	14
❏ **Elf Owl**—*Micrathene whitneyi*	25
❏ **Gambel's Quail**—*Callipepla gambelii*	16
❏ **Gila Woodpecker**—*Centurus uropygialis*	21
❏ **Great Horned Owl**—*Bubo virginianus*	23
❏ **Hooded Oriole**—*Icterus cucullatus*	9

Checklist and Scientific Names

	Page
❏ Lesser Nighthawk—*Chordeiles acutipennis*	27
❏ Loggerhead Shrike—*Lanius ludovicianus*	8
❏ Mockingbird—*Mimus polyglottos*	3
❏ Mourning Dove—*Zenaida macroura*	19
❏ Phainopepla—*Phainopepla nitens*	12
❏ Poor-will—*Phalaenoptilus nuttallii*	26
❏ Purple Martin—*Progne subis*	13
❏ Pyrrhuloxia—*Cardinalis sinuata*	11
❏ Red-tailed Hawk—*Buteo jamaicensis*	28
❏ Roadrunner—*Geococcyx californianus*	17
❏ Screech Owl—*Otus asio*	24
❏ Turkey Vulture—*Cathartes aura*	30
❏ Verdin—*Auriparus flaviceps*	15
❏ White-winged Dove—*Zenaida asiatica*	18